4 STEPS TO EMOTIONAL FREEDOM

How to be Happy Again After Painful Life Changes

CATH LLOYD

Book production by MysticqueRose Publishing Services LLC

ISBN: 978-1-3999-7362-5

CONTENTS

Acknowledgements

When I used to think about being an author, I always imagined it as a very solo activity, but I was very wrong. It takes a team of people, past and present, to develop a book with longevity and meaning. As I write, there are people in the background guiding me and challenging me on my ideas so that I write the best book I possibly can.

With this in mind, I would like to thank Porsché Mysticque Steele, CEO of MysticqueRose Publishing Services, and her team for all their hard work. Helping me put my daft ideas into some sort of order, the proofreader, the editors, the illustrator, and also the administrators co-ordinating the whole team. All the toing and froing that goes with the process and all doing our best to keep to the timeframe. Writing a book creates a lot of head scratching, brain ache, and excitement but also terrifying feelings of trying to produce something that I will always be proud of.

My family, fellow writing friends, and business colleagues are also an important part of this process to bounce ideas off of.

My husband, Nick, and children, Jess and Pete, helped to keep me grounded as a wife and a mum so that I don't get blown away by the otherwise self-centred process. I thank my husband for his unwavering love in the most difficult times we have been through as a family. My daughter Jess for her strength of character, support, and unwavering love when life events have taken us elsewhere. I thank my son, Pete, for always being supportive when I want to talk about his life-changing injury so that I can support other people. As a family, Nick, Jess, and Pete all want to help others get through their tough times so they don't have to struggle longer than they choose to, and this means being open and freely sharing information and some of the most difficult emotions, thoughts, and feelings. I would also like to thank the very first person who supported me when I began writing, proofreading for me, and having faith in my abilities, Fiona Hibbard, work colleague and friend.

I would also like to thank my late parents for the values they instilled in me at a very early age to support others and the strength of character that allows me to find a way around any situation. My dad and Joan, who was able to be self-honest about her gender. Even though this was a really tough process, at the time, it sent me on a journey of self-learning and understanding so that I could find my way through other tough times in my life. Without these tough times and my ability to learn and understand myself better, I wouldn't have been able to write this book with an open heart and share it with you all. Unfortunately, my parents never knew about this book, but I have faith that they are somewhere keeping a guiding eye on me.

I would like to thank my Uncle John, Uncle Loz, and Auntie Sue for their regular check-ins and support, especially since my parents have passed, and to my sister, Helen, for always being there.

Finally, I would like to thank the clients who were also an essential part of this book and allowed me to use their experiences to support my 4 Steps to Emotional Freedom theory. Thank you, ladies. You are all stars.

Lastly, I want to say thank you to you, for picking up this book. I hope it impacts you like it has done me to give you an transformative experience and help you change your life so that you can end sadness to restore happiness after a painful change.

Love and best wishes,

Cath Lloyd

Introduction

You never thought it would be like this.

You didn't think you would find this change in your life so difficult.

Everything that has occurred since then takes you by surprise. You're angry. You feel like all the burden is being placed on your shoulders and you're completely unappreciated and misunderstood. You don't know where to go from here, and at times, you feel like not going anywhere at all.

What you are experiencing is phase one of achieving emotional freedom. It might feel awful now, but I promise, you are right where you should be.

Any massive change in your life is likely to bring with it feelings of bereavement and grief. Bereavement and grief aren't just reserved for the finality of life. When we go through big changes like separation, chronic illness, and death, there will be some sort of loss attached to it, whether we are conscious of it or not.

Elisabeth Kübler Ross[1] talks about different phases of the cycle of change and loss in her 5 Stages of Grief – death and dying.

1. Denial
2. Anger
3. Bargaining
4. Depression
5. Acceptance

These five stages are fluid, meaning you may experience different stages several times before you reach the stage of acceptance. If you take a moment to really think about your life and what you are going through, experiencing these is perfectly normal. I hear so many clients who feel bewildered and ashamed of their difficult thoughts and feelings. I try to help them be kinder to themselves and more understanding of their circumstances.

As a daughter, wife, and mother, I am no different from anyone else. Like many others, I have been through extremely tough periods in my life, and I am not ashamed to say I struggled. I struggled with acknowledging the situations, accepting them, and understanding the emotional turmoil that came with both.

In 1987, my dad announced he was going to begin treatment for gender dysphoria. It took me a long time to understand the feelings I was having. I realised I was struggling to come to terms with difficult thoughts and feelings of uncertainty for our future as a family and understand why my dad's brain was playing tricks on him. I struggled with confused feelings of wanting to be supportive, but I was also frightened and wanted to run away. I felt guilty for my feelings because I knew other people were struggling with harder situations than this.

The thing was, I had no idea how to manage this massive change that had suddenly been thrust into my life. Up until that moment, life felt secure, unshakeable, and…normal.

---

1. Kübler-Ross, E. (1997). On death and dying: What the dying have to teach doctors, nurses, clergy, and their families. Simon & Schuster/Touchstone Book.

After a lot of false starts, it wasn't until I had a meltdown due to stress that I finally realised I had to start *managing* my difficult thoughts and feelings. What saved me was what I learnt about myself, acknowledging how I was feeling, and deciding I wanted something better for myself and the important people in my life. I started practising the skill of *self-honesty*. This helped me understand myself so I could begin to figure out why I was feeling the way I was and what I wanted differently.

Once I knew this, I could start working on how I was going to develop a range of tools and techniques to get me there and create new thinking habits.

Even though I struggled with my dad's decision to go through gender reassignment to become Joan, I now thank him. I thank him for being true to himself and becoming the person he knew he should be instead of hiding behind the façade of an alpha male. I thank him for the lessons I learnt about myself. It was this learning and understanding that helped me get through the second difficult change in my life.

In 2017, my 20-year-old son had a tragic mountain bike accident. He broke his neck and became a tetraplegic with severe life-changing injuries. I thought I knew what it felt like to have a broken heart, but this was much worse than anything I had experienced before. This put my emotional well-being, mental and physical health, and the strength of us as a family to the real test.

This book is a starting point and guide for those who are ready to start changing their life for the better, for those who are tired of the pain, the heartache, and the mental torture they are feeling. It is for those who want to find their new normal in life, those who want to get back to living life as best they can, and those who are fed up with playing the victim, who are tired of talking and want to take action instead.

Are you ready for this new start?

If you are, I am excited for you and want to share my **4 Steps to Emotional Freedom.**

Step 1: Discover Your Self-Honesty

Step 2: Gain Acceptance

Step 3: Find Your New Ways Forward

Step 4: Time for Action

This book will take you on a journey of discovery. It will challenge you, provoke you, and inspire you. You will experience emotional freedom instead of feeling as if you are being held ransom by those difficult thoughts and feelings that are making you:

Feel as if you lack control.

Feel guilt.

Feel isolated and left behind.

Miss your lust for life.

As you progress through this book, you will walk away equipped to learn and understand yourself, the variables in your relationships and the knowledge of how to change them for the better. You may already be practising some of these skills without realising them. Just *recognising* them will begin to give you a sense of security and control. Instead of wanting to throw your hands up in the air and yell, "I can't do this anymore!", you will be able to look at life objectively and with more patience for yourself and others. You will be able to see the future as an open door of possibility.

If you are fed up with making excuses and personal objections that are keeping you in victim mode, continue reading to learn how to achieve emotional freedom.

Attempting to work on yourself, find yourself, learn, and understand yourself takes time. Change doesn't occur quickly. It's an ongoing process. Often, we don't notice a positive or negative change unless it is something significant, but little by little, we are changing every day.

How many films or TV series have you watched when the characters seem perfectly rational?

Then suddenly, something extreme happens, perhaps in love, lust, jealousy, or trauma, and they behave like a totally different person – almost like Jekyll and Hyde. In times of great anxiety and stress, you can feel like a totally different person inside. You may be managing to control it to a certain extent. But, as time goes by, these Jekyll and Hyde characteristics may start to seep through your normally-reasonable demeanour. You can feel out of control. Instead of being in the driver's seat, you are controlled by this turmoil of loss, sadness, and frightening series of thoughts and feelings.

You can save yourself.

My 4-step methodology was developed after a combination of those two life-changing events. Learning more about my thoughts and feelings from the first event helped me start to manage the second. The second event was a different struggle and made me work deeper and more intensely to learn and understand my thoughts and feelings. The more you *learn and understand yourself*, the better equipped you are to manage the next difficult life experience you go through. I'm not suggesting you dwell on the negatives in your life. I believe you should make the most of life, but unfortunately, the cycle, the ups and downs, can get in the way. If you learn and understand more about yourself and your life, you are in a much better place to manage these ups, downs, and cycles – bringing in your coping strategies as and when you need them. Some you will use every day to maintain your level of normal. When you start to feel yourself sway, it is time to bring in these coping strategies to easily manage the situation.

In the creation of this book, I interviewed several ladies and walked them through the 4 Steps to Emotional Freedom process. This would allow me to clearly understand how personal concerns are reflected through thoughts, feelings, and behaviours and how the process supports them in their journey through massive change.

I met with Emily, Georgia, Vanessa, and Lizzy.

Emily was struggling with various rifts in her family and reconnecting with her brother who was going through gender reassignment.

Georgia was experiencing the build-up of family roles and responsibilities but also needed to take the helm of control because there was nobody else to do it. She felt like she was the only one capable of fulfilling the role. Along with taking control, she was also juggling a handful of other roles and responsibilities; her daughter needed extra support, taking care of her own health, and she was the main caregiver for her parents-in-law.

Vanessa was still grieving the sad death of her father but also the traumatic death of her mother. She had a full-time, high-pressure job and was also helping to support her aunt, who was at the end of her life.

Lizzy felt the pressures of caring for her family that had been building up over a few years. Her youngest child was diagnosed with a lifelong illness at the same time as the death of her beloved father. A few years later, her mother died whilst Lizzy was running a business.

You will be learning more about these ladies as you continue to read and will probably recognise some of yourself in them.

This book will give you:

1. A safe place to practice self-care and personal development.
2. Easy to understand methodology and logic.
3. The ability to revisit the knowledge time and time again.
4. A way to feel understood.

This doesn't mean you aren't going to have a series of personal objections along the way, and you may even experience your normal set of default coping strategies to pass the emotional pain of difficult thoughts and feelings. I assure you, the drive to want something better for yourself is the best starting point for anyone. It just takes time and patience.

Knowledge isn't power until you use it.

— Dale Carnegie

The Fallout
(Stages After Massive Change)

Though emotions and thoughts are closely connected, they differ. Unfortunately, we've been taught to tune out our emotions and, instead, concentrate on our thoughts and thought processes. The problem with this is our emotions impact our feelings, our mood, and our thoughts, which, in turn, impacts how we view the world around us. Our emotions drive every decision we make, whether we're conscious of it or not.

Paul Ekman was a leading psychologist and pioneer in studying emotion and its relationship to facial expressions. Ekman discovered there are 6 basic emotions – sadness, happiness, fear, anger, surprise, and disgust. These emotions not only drive us, but when mixed together, create a long list of more complex emotions, including love, grief, worry, guilt, and gratitude.

The interesting point here is these emotions are made up of 3 parts: subjective experiences, physiological responses, and behavioural responses.

All emotions start as a subjective experience depending on how a person responds to a situation. One person's loss of a loved one can give rise to the emotions of intense sadness but for another person, anger and regret. These emotions let us know exactly how we're feeling at that precise time.

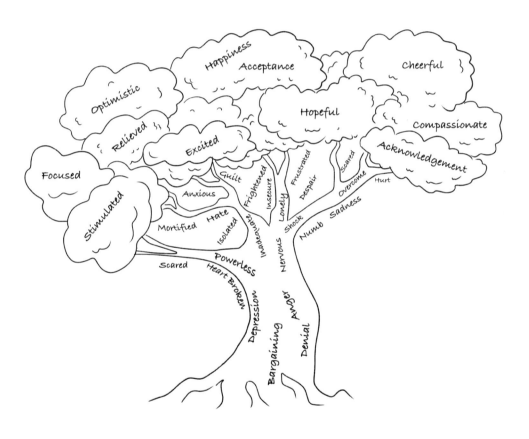

The physiological responses are automatic. They are the reaction of the nervous system to emotion, which controls our involuntary body responses, including our facial expressions, voice, and regulation of fight or flight.

Our internal reactions rapidly move into a behaviour response – the external expression of the situation, which lets others know exactly how we're feeling. It is the most basic of human communication systems.

Our perception of someone is generated from their emotions. When we're in a face-to-face conversation, our perception of a person will be influenced by their facial expressions and body language. If on the phone, we notice it in their voice.

Being able to understand yourself starts here. Learning to recognise your emotions, how they make you feel, and how they affect your mood will help you understand your reaction to situations you're in.

When we think about change in this way, it can help us focus and give us the opportunity to keep in check what is important to us. However, as we know, change over a short period of time can create anxiety and stress and, if unaddressed, can lead to depression and persistent depressive disorder, also known as dysthymia.

The more you understand the different stages of the change curve, the more you will realise you aren't the only one struggling. While in the depths of the bereavement cycle of change and loss, it can be a very lonely place. Our thoughts and feelings are personal, and you can't assume you know exactly what someone else is thinking and feeling, even by looking for clues in their facial expression, tone of voice, or body language. It can, however, be comforting to know you aren't the only one going through a very natural and common process. Knowing you are not alone can help you overcome some of the feelings of isolation, inadequacy, and guilt.

Throughout this chapter, I will be discussing the problems that can occur when managing and coming to terms with significant changes in our lives. I will also be introducing you to some of the difficulties Emily faced in her journey as she struggled through change.

As noted in the introduction, Elisabeth Kubler-Ross was the first person to research and plot out the guidelines for the bereavement and grief process you may go through:

- Denial (Avoidance, confusion, shock, elation, fear)
- Anger (Frustration, irritation, anxiety)
- Bargaining (Struggling to find meaning, reaching out to others, telling one's story)
- Depression (Overwhelmed, helplessness, hostility, flight)
- Acceptance (Exploring options, new plan in place, moving on)

According to her, this process is not set in stone and varies for everyone. The stages are determined by:

1. The severity of the loss/change
2. Circumstances surrounding the loss/change
3. Individual differences in:
   - Personalities
   - Temperament
   - Culture
   - Spiritual and religious beliefs
   - Upbringing

Denial

I am sure most of us have been told some terribly surprising news that has left us stunned, speechless, and almost gasping for breath while uttering:

"I don't believe it."

"Are you sure?"

"There must be a mistake."

Denial sounds very negative, but in fact, it's our body's natural way of protecting us from the truth, helping to spread out the feelings we are experiencing and the full impact of the situation. It causes our minds to be in a state of disbelief and gives us hope the news is incorrect. It causes in us a need for a second or even third opinion.

Denial causes the mind to pretend you aren't living in reality but in a preferred reality. At this stage, oftentimes, life makes no sense, and our mind creates thoughts of "Why us?" "Why now?" and "What have I done to deserve this?"

However, gradually, these feelings of loss eventually come to the surface, allowing you to start managing your grief and allowing the healing process to begin.

Emily was one of the first ladies I had the pleasure of interviewing. She explained,

"I was in total disbelief that my brother was serious about going through gender reassignment."

She had a very close bond with her brother when they were growing up. Even though her brother was the eldest sibling, he found it hard to defend himself against the bullies at school. Emily was protective and fought his battles for him. Subconsciously, the school bullies saw a weakness in him and acted on it. Her brother's feelings of helplessness against them welcomed his sister's defence, but this closeness between them meant it was difficult for him to open up to Emily about his desire for gender reassignment and also why Emily found it so hard to come to terms with his decision. The shock of the information set off an automatic reaction in Emily.

"I wanted to shake him and tell him he was being ridiculous."

Denial can cause us to physiologically respond in mysterious ways.

When my dad announced that he was going to start gender reassignment treatment, it was such a surprise. He had never shown any signs of wanting to be a woman. Granted, he was caring, kind, and supportive, but that was just his nature. I was so shocked my thought processes went into autopilot. I laughed until I noticed the hurt on his face and realised he was dead serious.

Both my and Emily's responses show that when in shock, our minds go into autopilot. They react in ways that may appear to be unreasonable, out of character, or even mean. At this stage, we have very little control over this automatic response, and this can result in a lot of hurt if a follow-up conversation about our reaction is ignored.

Anger

As a child, I was taught to control my anger, and I imagine others were too, which, in turn, causes anger to feel like a very strange emotion to some of us. Being able to process our anger and release it will help us move through this stage more quickly. A lot of people are frightened of their anger and may feel as if they won't be able to control themselves if they reveal it or are afraid it will never stop. The fact is, the ability to keep it under wraps means it is actually controlling you and creating more mental health and well-being issues. Holding in anger can leave you feeling as if there's nowhere to turn, that the ground has opened up, and life is running through your fingers like sand.

Emily was angry with her brother for keeping this information to himself for so long. What made it even worse was how close they were growing up. At times, Emily almost felt as if she had been betrayed and then later felt angry with herself for being selfish, thinking about how her brother's gender dysphoria would affect her.

It's at this stage you might be trying to place blame, find a cause, question your faith, or express something along the lines of, "It's always the good people who suffer."

The truth is, change, chronic illness, and fatal accidents happen in all walks of life to all sorts of people, good or bad, but it's what we choose to believe about it that can start to cloud our judgement.

During my son's recovery, the anger manifested but at different stages. The first bout reared its ugly head whilst out having a meal. I was angry at other customers for being drunk, laughing, and having a good time whilst my son was lying motionless on a ventilator in intensive care under constant surveillance. How dare they be out enjoying themselves when I was feeling heartbroken with no idea of what my son's future, our future, was going to hold.

My second bout of anger didn't come until a couple of weeks later when our son's second operation was cancelled for the second time due to his poor health. This time, it was directed towards his girlfriend and her parents for just being who they were, for beating me to his bedside on the morning of his second operation, and for being there when I couldn't be.

The third time I experienced anger, I directed it at my son. He was about four weeks in when he was moved to the isolation ward for Clostridium Difficile (C Diff.), a bacteria that is in our body all the time but can flare up as a reaction to taking antibiotics. This anger rose because of his obsession with a high-risk sport versus sticking with something less dangerous like golf. I vividly remember the ward rounds. One consultant, in particular, arrived with all his colleagues. He greeted me and asked how I was.

"I am so angry I could beat him to a pulp," I said.

A look of horror grew on the faces of the medical staff. They couldn't believe I would say such a thing whilst my son lay critically ill next to me. The consultant turned away from his medical records, looked at me, and cooly said, "You are entitled to think that. You are his mother."

He understood. While the other medical staff still had to learn this possible reaction and human nature during trauma, I wondered how many times he had heard this.

Even though anger is an uncomfortable set of emotions to go through, it's important. This is what self-honesty feels like. Being able to express your emotions helps release them instead of allowing them to eat you up inside.

Bargaining

"Bargaining is a defence against the feelings of helplessness experienced after a loss. It happens when people struggle to accept the reality of the loss and the limits of their control over the situation." —*Sabrina Romanoff, PSYD.*

There are two types of bargaining: bargaining in the present and bargaining in the past.

Bargaining in the present – The desire to act in a particular way, believing it will help you feel better or believing the situation will miraculously improve.

Bargaining in the present during my son's injury revolved around thinking I would be able to fix the situation because I was his mother. I had fixed everything else in his life for him so far, hadn't I? I spent a lot of time reaching out to the higher spirits and using essential oils to generate more nerve impulses in his body after his operation to secure his neck. He hadn't severed his spinal cord so the nerves could regenerate, or so I thought.

Bargaining over the past – wishing you could go back so the present would be different, so the change/loss would have been prevented.

This may look and feel like:

- Guilt and shame over thoughts and feelings
- Feelings of insecurity, fear, or anxiety
- Ruminating over what could have been
- Holding yourself responsible
- Punishing yourself
- Judging yourself and others
- Making comparisons
- Trying to predict the future
- Wishing or praying for a different outcome
- Thinking and saying, "What if?" or "If only"

Bargaining in the past happened quickly. If my son had stuck with golf, this never would have happened. If he had stayed living near home, it never would have happened. If he hadn't gone out riding that day, it never would have happened.

I felt like I almost wished this to happen or knew it would happen. I felt it was my fault. The times other spectators at Enduro Mountain Bike races asked me if I was frightened of what my son did on his bike and what could happen, I would reply, "Of course, but you get used to it. If something happens, I will be there to pick up the pieces."

Not in my wildest dreams did I imagine this.

I thought his dislocated shoulder would be the worst of it.

If I hadn't said that, he would have come off his bike like so many other times before and rolled his way out of trouble. But this time he wasn't so lucky.

Depression

"Depression is a common mental disorder. Globally, it is estimated that 5% of adults suffer from the disorder. It is characterised by persistent sadness and a lack of interest in pleasure in previously rewarding or enjoyable activities. It can also disturb sleep and appetite."

Depression can lead to feelings of emptiness, feeling numb, living life in a fog, feeling as if you are outside of your body, being overwhelmed or secluding yourself. In severe cases, depression can lead to feelings and thoughts of suicide or self-harm.

Everyone experiences the severity of this change curve in different ways, but it's important to understand the impact it can have on your body, mind, and soul.

Emily experienced depression after her, now, sister tried to take her own life after coming out into the open with her gender dysphoria. This depression lasted for a year. Emily desperately wanted to look after her sister but felt she didn't have the mental or emotional capacity to while trying to take care of herself.

For the majority of people, there will be a turning point that is determined by many things, including how much you personally want to change the way you think and feel. With determination and the natural process of the stages, you *will* move into acceptance.

Acceptance

Over time and with the right help and support, you'll gradually begin to notice different thoughts and feelings seeping through because your emotions begin stabilising. However, there is a balance between forcing a change in your thoughts and feelings and allowing yourself to go through the natural bereavement process of change and loss.

During the acceptance stage, you will begin to come to terms with the situation and realise you will be okay.

You will still have your bad days, and you may even feel some guilt for being happy again as the tragedy isn't at the forefront of your mind all the time. On the good days, you will start seeing your new future and adjusting to the reality of the situation, the fog will begin to lift, and you'll want to start socialising again.

Emily began to accept her sister's decision to change gender after spending a lot of time talking with her and understanding her needs and wants to live a truthful life. She soon began to realise she hadn't lost her brother. She now had a sister to support and welcome into her life.

There is no wrong or right way of going through your bereavement process. It should be seen as fluid – you will move forward and backward, maybe many times. Even when you feel as if you are on the other side and safely in full acceptance, on occasions, such as anniversaries or holidays, you may find yourself digressing back into fleeting times of anger, bargaining, or depression.

Re-entering the reality of the situation without forcing yourself too early is really important and may help you be:

- supportive
- in control
- organised
- a better person
- stronger
- resilient
- capable
- less weak
- more like your usual self

Where are you in your journey of the bereavement cycle of change and loss? (Tick one.)

- Denial ☐
- Anger ☐
- Bargaining ☐
- Depression ☐
- Acceptance ☐

Do you feel as if you have moved up and down through the change curve?

Mark on the curve where you feel you currently are.

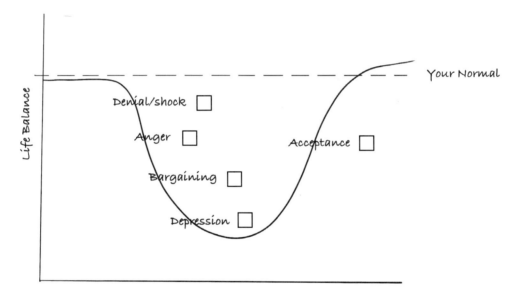

Bereavement Cycle of Change and Loss

My journey through the bereavement change curve was a very fluid affair when my son broke his neck.

In the beginning, we weren't aware of the extent of the damage to his vertebrae and spinal cord. My husband and I thought he would be in the hospital for a few days and then we would bring him home to recuperate.

Once at the hospital, we were quickly ushered into the ward. Our family, the staff, and my son, all tried to keep a positive outlook on the situation expressing things like,

"It'll be ok." "You'll be back to your usual self." "We'll do everything we can to get you well again."

What did these words really mean?

When I look back, we were trying to make the best of a traumatic situation, trying to look on the bright side. We had hope.

While my husband broke down, I tried to keep in control, stay positive and hopeful; hopeful the surgeons would work miracles to repair his C3 vertebrae, releasing his spinal cord so it would revive and allow our son to gain full recovery.

When our son was waiting to be transferred to the spinal unit, we were told, "They are wonderful there. They will work miracles with him."

I didn't recognize I was in a depressive state. I thought it was normal to have to manage feelings of dissociation from what was going on around me, poor sleep, and loss of appetite.

Some days, I lost track of whether or not I was communicating with my family, like my husband, who was at home running his business, and our daughter at university, who was looking after our dogs.

On the really desperate days, when I felt total, emotional pain, I considered self-harm. I didn't know what else to do with the pain. I hadn't experienced anything like this before.

" *If I cut myself, the pain will be better. If I bury myself in the snow and freeze, all this pain will go away,"* were the thoughts running through my mind.

Gradually, I separated the bad weeks, days, hours, and moments out and started to experience fleeting moments when I could smile and be happy. This, I knew, would gradually turn into happiness.

When we gradually began to understand what life for our son was going to entail, we could start to plan. We gradually started to plan a future for our son and started to get some kind of order and routine.

When I felt helpless and back to square one of denial and shock, this was when I had the bad days. I remember sitting in the spinal unit, flipping through the magazines of all the positive things people with a spinal injury were doing now, two, five, and ten years after their injury. In every single magazine, I read about paraplegics. It was all the magazines talked about. But where were all the tetraplegics? What are they doing? Nothing, according to these magazines.

At the goal-setting meetings with the clinical psychotherapist, consultant, and other doctors on the team, we were told our son could still have a full and active life. I remember trying to control the venom in my voice as I spoke.

"He can't even get into bed and just have an afternoon cuddle with his girlfriend. How is that having a normal, full, and active life?"

There was no reply, just a look of disinterest and discomfort from the goal-setting team. I was told I wasn't being realistic.

How can you be realistic when you don't know what reality is going to look like anymore?

In truth, realism comes from research, digging deep into yourself to discover what you want and who you want to be in your life. This is what you will draw from to create your new reality.

Remember, any change brings problems, but those problems bring goals and objectives that are unknown. It's how we decide to manage life after the change that will decide our future, the successes, and joys waiting for us.

> **The secret of change is to focus all of your energy not on fighting the old, but on building the new.**
>
> — Socrates

The Evolution
(How Change Manifests Itself)

Change is a continual process happening all around us, and you will see this as a progression or a decline depending on what sort of change you are experiencing.

The Age UK Charity[2] discussed the evidence from research by The Disconnected Mind project regarding the contribution of genetics and our environment in how we manage change as we age. "They discovered that approximately 24% … of change between childhood and older age (age 70) is due to genetic influences. This means that environmental influences make a larger contribution, at approximately 76%." Environmental influences can include:

- Lifestyle choices
- Our upbringing
- Education levels
- Our own personality types
- Our belief system

It's important to remember we all respond differently; therefore, we will adjust differently.

It is also important to recognise that struggling with significant change is normal and nothing to be ashamed of, nothing to feel guilty about, nothing

---

2. Do Genes Influence Thinking Skills. Age UK. (2022, September 20). https://www.ageuk.org.uk/information-advice/health-wellbeing/mind-body/staying-sharp/thinking-skills-change-with-age/genes-and-thinking-skills/

to feel you should dismiss. However, holding onto the negative emotions of change may be stopping you from embracing healing.

The minute details of our own individual thoughts and feelings can create a massive struggle within ourselves as we process, ruminate over, and battle with them. When we're in the middle of significant change, we too often tell ourselves:

"I'm being silly."

"I'm being selfish."

"There are far worse things happening around the world than what's happening to me."

Change is inevitable, so why does change become something we find so difficult to manage?

Change is constant in our lives, but at times, it's:

- Unexpected
- Traumatic
- Has us juggling roles and responsibilities that have built up over time
- A combination of all of these

"Association of Stressful Life Events with Psychological Problems"[3] a community-based study states:

"Difficult adjustment is usually shown in children as acting up or acting out. In adults, it can be shown through sadness, crying, worry, trouble sleeping and withdrawal."

The report goes on to say, "Most people can overcome these symptoms with some form of therapy, not necessarily medication. However, this could be prolonged by a combination of stressors that are present in life and if left untreated can create more serious disorders such as PTSD, bipolar,

---

3. Akbar Hassanzadeh, Zahra Heidari, Awat Feizi, Ammar Hassanzadeh Keshteli, Hamidreza Roohafza, Hamid Afshar, Payman Adibi, "Association of Stressful Life Events with Psychological Problems: A Large-Scale Community-Based Study Using Grouped Outcomes Latent Factor Regression with Latent Predictors", Computational and Mathematical Methods in Medicine, vol. 2017, Article ID 3457103, 12 pages, 2017. https://doi.org/10.1155/2017/3457103

depression and should be taken seriously because it is associated with the increase in self-harm and suicide."

Let's face it, life can get complicated and becomes even more complicated as we get older, which is where the stressors in life can really start to tip the balance in our emotional and mental well-being. There is no doubt any big change will disrupt your life.

Very quickly, life can become unrecognisable due to these stressors:

- Social Life - rifts in friendships, moving
- Family – Births, deaths, family conflict, separation/divorce
- Finances – Buying a house, losing or changing jobs, retirement, separation, chronic illness
- Health – Acute or chronic illness, injury from an accident
- A combination of these

When you are on the outside looking in, it can be easy to recognise why people struggle with coping mechanisms and have a difficult time staying in control – a poor diet, dependency, poor lifestyle choices, and withdrawal from friends, family, and responsibilities.

Some might say they are "burying their head in the sand," but when you are in the thick of it, it's hard to organise your thought processes and understand the turmoil of feelings whilst still running your home, going to work, and making sure everything is ticking along smoothly. A big change will cause you to put up your defences, and you either respond with flight or fight.

Change can make us face rejection, failure, and loss but also celebrate triumph and accomplishment. The more we face change and engage with it, the more we learn, understand, and grow.

Though it may not be to an outsider, this is very real for you, and making excuses while pushing it aside may make your thoughts and feelings subside a little or for a while, but they will rear their ugly heads again and again until you begin to start addressing them appropriately.

Subconsciously, our hearts, bodies, and minds are still processing the information as they quietly work away in the background, trying to understand why we are thinking and feeling this way, making excuses, and trying to protect ourselves. You see, our minds don't know what is real or not. It's the stories we create that keep them alive, feeding our belief systems whilst our thinking and feeling habits grow stronger.

You may be saying:

"How do I know I am struggling?"

"I have been having these thoughts and feelings for years. How do I know what is real and what isn't?"

"I can't remember when I felt any different."

When you are caught up in difficult change, you are inside your own head, focusing on the situation. You may be thinking about how you can fix the problems, stay in control, and juggle all your roles and responsibilities. It's easy to put your thoughts and feelings at the bottom of your "To Do List" and you at the bottom of important people in your life.

When the real thoughts and feelings start to come to the surface, it's quicker and easier to ignore them than to address them, making it difficult to know which are real and which are imagined. After a while, this sort of thinking becomes a habit, and you get used to having these thoughts and feelings, suppressing the ones you don't like for the ones that help you function.

It is time to start addressing your feelings.

Let's begin coming face to face with all those difficult thoughts and feelings you have been avoiding.

Symptoms can vary widely from one person to the next.

If you are reading this, you must be interested in improving your life in some way. The first step is to be honest with yourself.

Below is a list of symptoms that are often experienced when dealing with change. Please use this checklist to look at the symptoms you're experiencing. Tick the ones that apply to you.

- Sleep – vivid dreams and continual feelings of tiredness whether sleeping longer than average or experiencing disturbed sleep patterns
- Weight – weight gain or weight loss even though your diet may not have altered much, lack of appetite, overeating
- Social life – wanting to hide away from your usual social hangouts or a big change in your socialising habits
- Concentration and decision-making skills
- Craving unhealthy lifestyle choices – unhealthy foods, drinks, drugs
- Poor self-care regimens
- Extremes in your usual exercise routine
- Wanting to or crying for no reason
- Unusual feelings of self-harm and thoughts of suicide
- Need to be in control or the superhero or feeling out of control
- Intimacy – a need for more or less connectivity in your personal relationships
- Irritability, anger, frustration
- Headaches, muscle pain, digestive problems

This massive list of symptoms could become even more serious the longer the symptoms are ignored, resulting in heart or immune problems. We live lives of hierarchical needs, and when we go through difficult change it will have a knock-on effect in other areas of our lives. Take a look at Maslow's Hierarchy of Needs below.

Maslow's Hierachy of Needs

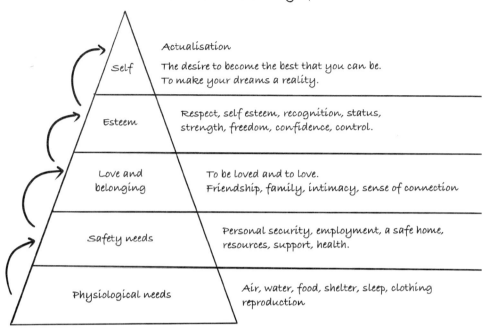

We need our very basic needs met before we can move up to the next level of progression. The more confident and comfortable we are, the higher up the pyramid we become. But if our boat is rocked, so to speak, we are out of our comfort zone and may slide back down to a lower level. It is only when we get to the top of the pyramid that we have real control over our lives and as individuals. We live our lives moving up and down the different hierarchy levels, experiencing the effects of this in our thoughts and feelings but never really understanding the effect this can have on our lives, which is why if issues are left unaddressed, these symptoms can influence other areas of our lives so easily.

As I mentioned earlier, I was able to work with several ladies through the 4 Steps to Emotional Freedom.

All these ladies have experienced some very tough times that revolved around their families.

This might sound pretty normal for most households, but what really stood out with all of these ladies was the continual build-up of their roles and responsibilities, the feelings of lack of respect, and several unexpected incidents happening at the same time. It was hard to understand why these things were happening, and they felt helpless, causing them to grasp at a sense of control. They went into a state of being needed, which met their own needs but built up the weight upon their existing roles and responsibilities.

My symptoms varied when struggling to totally accept my dad's transition to Joan versus my son's tragic mountain bike accident.

In the first instance, I felt I had my feelings under control. As my life developed, so did my family and a full-time teaching job. However, juggling life and my difficult thoughts and feelings started to take their toll. I was experiencing a lot of headaches and sciatic pain, trying to be a superhero at work and at home while still managing to find time to go to the gym to keep the perfect figure.

The day I turned 40, I felt like an 80-year-old, and it frightened me. All I could think was, *If I was feeling like this at the age of 40, what would life be like for me even if I did manage to reach the age of 80?*

When my son had his accident, I had very different symptoms, and it was also a very different situation. This was my son, my own flesh and blood, the child I carried in my womb and gave birth to. We were thrown into something totally unexpected.

That first night, my husband quickly broke down. As I held him in my arms, he sobbed and said, "Our son is broken." Life was going to be an unknown, and for how long, we didn't know.

We clung to what the professional told us, "With an injury like this, the majority of people in twelve months' time will be living the life they had at the time of their injury."

You hear what you want to hear, disregarding the rest. We were clinging to the miracle of hope. The miracle was this professional would be correct, and our son would be walking and ready to get back on his mountain bike again. This, however, was only the start of the journey for our son and us as a family.

Between looking after both my parents and keeping my business ticking along whilst also writing my book, *When Dad Became Joan*, my life was already a juggling act. But in an instant, it all changed. The juggling act suddenly became a whole lot more complicated. Four days a week, I looked after my parents, then took a 288-mile journey up to Edinburgh and then Glasgow to see our son over the weekends.

Our daughter convinced her landlord and housemates to have our dogs with her on the weekends. This gave her much-needed comfort with the unknown regarding her brother and the lack of parental support she was going to have to endure.

The unknown left me either feeling blank or with a head full of wild thoughts and feelings – anger, frustration, sorrow, sadness, and heartbreak. My child was broken. Why him? Why now? What's going to happen? How's it going to happen? How long is it going to take? How are we going to manage to get through this? How is our son going to get through this? So many questions and no answers except, "It's going to take time." and "We will have to wait and see."

Hum…

I felt helpless, so naturally, I put my practical self into action like so many others when they don't know what else to do.

I was so caught up in my own head, I neglected the other important people in my life, in my son's life.

On the flip side, I didn't want the all-important person in my son's life, his girlfriend, around. She was taking up my space and time with him, and she probably thought the exact same about me. But, like so many other difficult conversations that should have been, we never discussed this, so it just reverberated around in my head, making me angrier and angrier.

The innocent people who didn't know what was going on in my personal life were the object of my resentment – built-up anger, frustrations, the unknown. I resented the fun they were having – that they could chatter and laugh freely without a big weight pushing them down into the earth. How could they not see I was in pain, a pain so vast it filled the space around me? Every thought and feeling consumed each breath and filled the air as I exhaled. The emotional pain was so great in this first year after my son's accident, I vividly remember two moments when I didn't know what to do with it and considered self-harm.

It was the only way I thought the pain would diminish.

We all manage these situations differently.

Where are you on your journey through significant change?

Did the significant change happen a long while back?

Has it only just started?

Are you now ready to start addressing this change?

Is it still too painful to address?

Can you see a significant change on the horizon?

Wherever you are on your journey, it is okay.

It's very easy for others to tell you what you need to do and when, but the bereavement cycle of change and loss happens at a different rate and for different reasons for all of us. You have to be ready, and only you know when the time is right.

However, it is important to consider a few things at this stage.

How are you feeling about your current thoughts and feelings?

Are you feeling stuck or are you feeling as if you are moving in a positive direction?

Are you okay with being where you are in the bereavement cycle of change and loss?

How is it affecting your emotional, mental, and physical health?

How is this affecting other areas of your life – your relationships, work, and decision-making skills?

I am asking you these questions to help you start developing an understanding of your journey and yourself.

When I began my research for this book, I had a long list of possible ladies to talk to about being a part of the project. However, it became very apparent which of the ladies were willing to start a conversation about their difficult change and who could cope emotionally with the 4-Step Methodology to Emotional Freedom as life continued to challenge them. Only the ladies who were ready to take on the challenge were able to complete the course to emotional freedom, beginning their journey to restoring the peacefulness to live a confident life with vitality.

If you are not ready to start addressing the trauma of what you're thinking and feeling, it may be too painful to talk about it and delve in deeply. And yes, it is hard, really hard at times. Take it from someone who has been there and dealt with it, but you have to be ready.

To manifest change there are a set of cogs that need to be in place for the wheels to start turning so you can manage your change. Each cog will have a different role. You are fed up with thinking and feeling the way you are and want something better for yourself. You are ready to embrace and make the time to focus on a new way of thinking. You are ready to start putting yourself at the top of your priority list instead of at the bottom.

I can guarantee there will be barriers and hurdles that pop into your path. Life doesn't always run smoothly. You'll have to negotiate with them and reason with yourself to find the best resolution so you can continue your journey to emotional freedom. It's highly likely you will relapse. This generally happens when you find the process tough and feel it's too difficult to work on yourself. Relapse is also common when you start to feel a lot better about yourself. During this period of time, you will start to find excuses and start to think of others' needs before your own.

Even when the 4-Step Methodology to Emotional Freedom becomes tough, I believe you are worth investing in your future and those dreams of living your new normal. Are you willing to step outside the comfort zone of your habitual thoughts and feelings?

"Life will only change when you become more committed to your dreams than you are to your comfort zone.

— Bill Cox, bass guitarist for Jimi Hendrix"

The Roadblocks (Your Personal Objections)

It's how we decide to manage life after a significant change that will decide our future, the success and joys waiting for us.

Whether it is to make life more exciting, peaceful, secure, or less tedious, we all crave change. However, change can also make us feel nervous or anxious because it is unknown. Even if life isn't exactly how we want it, we usually find ourselves following some kind of routine. We form habits, which means we know what to expect and this can make us feel safe.

As I mentioned in the previous chapter, I spoke to many ladies to find out if they were a good fit to work with me on my 4 Steps to Emotional Freedom. While many were receptive to the idea of restoring happiness, others were hesitant and gave excuses for not wanting to take part in something that could be life-changing. It may seem logical to use the support around you, but our minds work in mysterious ways. It can be hard to connect with difficult thoughts and feelings, like you are organising a headful of spaghetti when all you really want is to restore the peace.

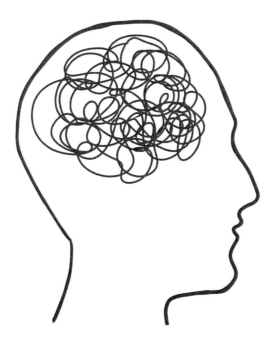

When we're given the opportunity to make a positive change, it can be difficult. Our heart and our head conflict:

One wants change and the other wants to keep things familiar.

One wants something better and the other wants to stay comfortable.

One is going through challenging emotions and the other doesn't want to face it.

The ladies who didn't make our first conversation told me they forgot, were too busy, or had personal issues that took priority.

Were these legitimate reasons or just excuses?

To clarify:

Legitimate – *Conforming to law or rules. Able to defend with logic or justification and is valid.*

Excuses – *To justify, to seek logic to lessen the blame. A reason or explanation to justify a fault or offence.*

When I was struggling to come to terms with my dad's decision to change gender, I was making the same excuses. They seemed legitimate at the time, but when I look back, I realise I was delaying what I really wanted. I was scared of myself, thoughts and feelings I had to come to terms with. It seemed legitimate to blame my dad for my struggle with his decision. It seemed legitimate to play the victim. Back in 1987, I didn't know anyone who had changed gender. Even now, I am only just hearing of trans issues in my close circle of friends.

These excuses may often be called Escape Coping Mechanisms. You find ways to avoid making any significant change to the situation or to the way you're feeling:

- I'm too tired.
- It's too upsetting.
- It's everyone else's fault.
- I forgot.
- Something else far more important came up.
- I just can't face it.

These thoughts are processed in our subconscious with automatic responses to delay what we know we need to do deep down.

Why would we want to put ourselves through even more pain than we're already experiencing?

To a certain extent, it can be easier to keep going through the pain we know and understand than to put ourselves through something that could be even worse. Therefore, we will argue we are "Okay with how we are." We might show defensiveness to any other suggestions and deem it unnecessary for any change to be made.

It's easier to keep using delay tactics, but eventually, we will get to the stage when issues have to be addressed. This is when either the emotional pain is just too hard to bear any longer or there are no more logical excuses available to us.

Protecting ourselves is what human beings are so good at. That's why we have been able to adapt and overcome some of the most horrific tragedies in the history of mankind.

This begs the question, are we putting our happiness on the back burner and leaving our watering can of self-love half full, jeopardising our levels of happiness, but still giving to others for the sake of an "easier" life in the moment?

If we are putting others before ourselves, again, we're keeping our watering can of self-love half full at the risk of running it down to empty.

If you can't run your car on an empty tank, how can you live a wonderful, fulfilled, and happy life without nurturing yourself? But nurturing yourself means coming to terms with and confronting difficult situations. This is going to be hard, emotionally painful, and bring to the surface negative thoughts and feelings you have buried deep inside of yourself for, perhaps, many years. In other words, by using avoidance and making excuses, you are playing a game with your personal wellness.

Georgia was the second lady I interviewed. She welcomed the opportunity to discuss her thoughts and feelings but also found it extremely difficult to go against her nature to work issues out silently and within her own head.

The process of keeping conversations confidential is always important when supporting others with their issues, and finding the right conditions, such as being out of earshot of family, to be able to do this can be challenging at times. The main objective was to support Georgia in her feelings of wanting to be in control, wanting things to be different, and feeling left behind or stuck.

Georgia was faced with the difficulties of supporting her ageing family members whilst also having to be mindful of her own health issues and her daughter's. As you can imagine, it was a large burden to bear, and she was doing her utmost to juggle all of these roles and responsibilities to keep family life running smoothly. The main issue she struggled with was giving away her time when others could have taken some of the responsibility. Others in the family had full-time jobs, and Georgia didn't, and this ultimately led to resentment. She felt as if she was being taken advantage of, misused, almost abused, and treated as if she had nothing else to do. She was beginning to feel as if she was neglecting her own home and self and found it really difficult to support her daughter as much as she wanted and needed to.

When Georgia was bargaining with herself, she felt as though she had no choice but to take on all the responsibility because of family dynamics and work commitments, so she decided to just "get on with it." However, the situation became worse when her sister-in-law moved away, making it difficult to pop in to see her mother.

It's important to note that Georgia isn't judgemental. She doesn't like to gossip and expects the same from others. However, this value she was holding stretched her, giving rise to feelings of resentment towards her sister-in-law and even, at times, her husband, who was still grieving the death of his father, which meant his mother needed extra support – an additional struggle for him. Georgia needed to gently support her husband in his bereavement process, but this was a fine balance, reminding him that Georgia and his mother both needed support as well.

On top of the loss of her father-in-law, her feelings for her sister-in-law were hard to manage. Georgia felt she was being left as the main caregiver for her mother-in-law with little communication between them. The day her sister-in-law moved was a big blow to the whole family and a traumatic event for Georgia's mother-in-law. Georgia soon felt the burden of the unspoken expectation of taking on extra roles and responsibilities of caring for her in-law. There was a constant feeling of anger that rapidly grew into something bigger, leaving Georgia with months of depression.

"The world is still going round and round. I'm still stuck," she said.

What became very apparent in our first week of working together was how quickly Georgia addressed a lot of the issues and was gradually building boundaries.

She voiced how much of her mother-in-law's care she would be responsible for each week, factoring in visits from other family members. During this time, Georgia decided to start a small creative business. This not only met Georgia's creative needs, giving her a sense of purpose and something to take her mind off other matters, but she now had deadlines and timelines to keep, changing family dynamics and gaining respect from her mother-in-law, which made life a lot easier.

She is an exceptionally caring person who likes to keep everyone happy, but this can come at an expense. On one hand, she was struggling with her own conscience around wanting to be supportive. On the other hand, they were not her parents so why should she be taking up the majority of the burden? She knew her parents-in-law needed care and support but could foresee how demanding this would become. How was she to reason between what was logical and illogical? How could her brain process the differences and arrive at an answer?

Her mind reeled back and forth about what she should do and why. Gradually, by reasoning with this argumentative thought process, she found her answer and resolve.

This was just like the arguments inside my head when my dad made the decision to undergo gender reassignment.

This is my dad, and I love him and want to be supportive, BUT, I'm scared and want to run away.

When faced with a change, we often reach the dilemma of pushing it to the back of our mind versus addressing it and sorting it out – coming to terms with it. However, this will eventually result in a day when the safety catch on the door can't take the pressure any longer, bursting open and spilling out all that is stuffed inside.

How do you change a life of avoidance that will generate not only a great deal of emotional pain but also relentless fatigue, feelings of lack of direction, anger, and more?

How much do you want to change it?

And who do you turn to for the right support?

"

Nothing can bring you happiness except yourself

— Ralph Waldo Emerson

"

4 Steps To Emotional Freedom (The Method)

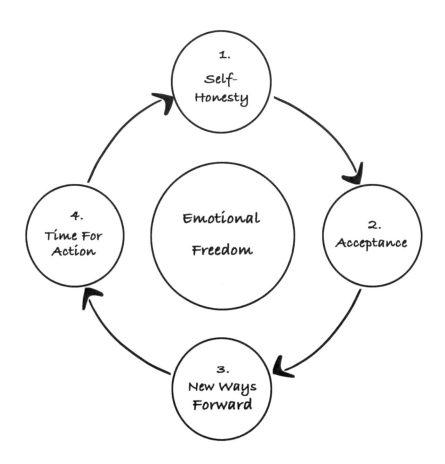

I realise you might be shouting at me,

"It's okay for you, but you don't know how I feel!"

"Your experience is different from mine!"

"This change I need to make isn't as easy as you say it is!"

You're absolutely right. My experiences of difficult change are probably different from yours. I would never tell you otherwise.

But what I do know is it's difficult to put your hand on your heart and be totally honest with yourself.

I also know it's hard to admit to the difficult thoughts and feelings, the guilt, the shame, and the massive mixture of secondary emotions that come along with them.

I never said it would be easy.

As you have been reading, you probably recognise I have had similar negativity, obstructions, and personal objections just like you. I put my hand up and admit I had a lot of false starts as well, but I wrote this book because I know; I have felt it, experienced it, thought it, and tried to avoid it.

We all know the hardest part of any change is taking the first step, but there is another hard part. You know you need to make a change, and you know why, but the second massive step is being totally committed to making this change, making change 100% with no turning back. It's at this stage you know you want to reach that pot of gold, the better life, the happiness you have been missing, to restore the calm and peace in your life. As you start your journey to emotional freedom, there will be barriers that get in your way – some larger than others, but I assure you, you will find a way around them.

To help you do this, I want to introduce you to my 4 Steps to Emotional Freedom. This methodology is based on 4 basic stages:

1. Self-honesty
2. Acceptance
3. New Ways Forward
4. Time For Action

Amongst these four steps, is an array of different activities you can use to support yourself in finding your way through the process. Each activity is geared toward where you are in the different stages of your change-making process and how you react to them.

People will often ask how long it will take and what the process is. It all depends on:

- Where you are with your thoughts and feelings.
- How far away you are from your end goals.
- What coping mechanisms you already have.
- What has been working for you?
- Your personal objections.
- The support network you have.
- How deep-rooted your thoughts and feelings are.
- The nature of the issues you're wanting to address.
- Your personality.
- How focused you are on wanting significant change in your life.

I want you to have a great experience and help motivate and inspire you to create very clear outcomes for your future. To achieve this, we need to delve deep into places that may have been ignored for many months or even years. This delving deep is going to be emotional, tiring, even exhausting, and intense. When I begin helping someone new, I am starting with a blank canvas. I ask a lot of questions to learn and paint a very clear picture of you. When Leonardo Da Vinci painted the Mona Lisa, he thought long and hard about what he wanted to convey. What emotions was he trying to invoke?

Unlike Leonardo Da Vinci, I am not trying to provoke a mystery. I am trying to unravel it. I need to have a clear picture so I have a definite starting point of what has come before and where you are currently heading.

When you picked up this book, what did you want it to help you resolve?

How do you want to be feeling and thinking?

What do you want life to give you?

If you don't have it in your mind yet, that's okay. We don't all have it straight away. That's why it's important to start with where you are today.

What does today look like to you?

What thoughts are coming up for you?

What emotions are you feeling?

The 4 Steps to Emotional Freedom is a system that can be used in any situation you are feeling stuck in and unsure of which way to go. It will give you a direction to work with and help you to start finding the answers you're looking for. However, following the 4 Steps to Emotional Freedom isn't a one-cycle process to achieve great results. To achieve long-lasting change and reach your long-term goals, you need to go through the process several times. How many times? I cannot say because each person's journey is as an individual and will depend on:

Your starting point.

Your end goal.

Your motivation to make changes.

The complexities of past experiences and limiting beliefs.

Working with this system will become a natural process, and you will be so accustomed it will result in an automatic way of thinking and problem-solving. This is a very fluid process, and you may find yourself jumping between the steps. Though this may happen, you still need to start at the beginning.

STEP 1: Establish your Self-honesty.

To be able to delve deep into the core of overcoming the difficult change you are managing, it's important to start practising self-honesty. For me, it's like putting my hand on my heart and connecting with what's really going on with my thoughts and feelings. The reason this can be frightening is because you will search through the dark and dingy passageways of your mind looking for the reasons why – almost like a private investigator.

We would rather protect ourselves than come face-to-face with what we are really thinking and feeling.

This step may generate feelings of guilt and shame, and it goes against what our ego is telling us.

It will create a long succession of argumentative conversations within us, causing us to hold our hand up and admit we were wrong.

An "authentic life" is the new buzz phrase that many people don't truly understand the meaning of or are willing to live by. Being authentic allows you to be truthful to yourself and others to live an honest life.

If you want to live an authentic life, then practising self-honesty is a necessity to finding the answers you're looking for.

When I finally decided I was fed up with fighting the losing battle of victim mode over my dad's decision to change gender, I literally put my hand on my heart. As I sat like this, I wrote everything I was thinking and feeling. I wrote in no particular order – just what was coming to me. I downloaded. With this download came the guilt and shame of what I had been harbouring for many, many years. I started to delve into the dark and dingy passageways of my mind.

This self-honesty was a struggle, and I felt emotionally hurt.

With this came a lot of crying.

Cleansing.

There was so much to process I felt exhausted, but it also felt good to be able to let go of it. Since I'd written it down, I still had the information in case I needed to revisit it. The important point here is, it was out of my head, freeing up space for other things, better things.

When you hold on to so many strong emotions, thoughts, and feelings, it creates a lot of anxiety and stress. You not only hold it in your thoughts but also in your body. Perhaps you've noticed this in yourself.

Where are the aches and pains in your body?

How is your body managing daily life?

How are your digestion and gut responding?

When you wake up in the morning, are you raring to go, or is it hard work getting out of bed?

Have your life choices changed?

These are some of the areas in your life that can be affected by carrying all the baggage of difficult change. Being in tune with your body and starting to notice these will help you learn and understand how your body is responding to what you are holding on to.

ACTION STEP: In writing, download what is on your mind. Put your hand on your heart and answer the above questions.

STEP 2: Accept your Emotions, Feelings, and Thoughts

Practising the skill of self-honesty, along with answering the questions, will help you accept the difficult change you're in. Start asking yourself those difficult questions you would rather avoid – those questions that make you cringe and want to run away. Revisit your written download and investigate the unanswered areas by asking:

Is this what I am really thinking and feeling or is it something else?

Why am I thinking and feeling like this?

How is this a benefit to me and others?

How is this going to help the situation?

Take the time to delve deep and write it all down to free up your head space so you can revisit it when you need to.

When I was really struggling with the deep emotional pain in my heart after my son's mountain bike accident, I had to go through this process. I vividly remember wanting to end the pain.

The first time was about two weeks after the initial accident. It was a sunny day in September. My daughter was with me. We had gone to the hospital early to see him before his second operation. In ITU, like most wards, there was a restriction to three visitors per bed. My daughter made a diversion to the toilet and was due to follow me into the ward. I arrived at my son's bedside to find his girlfriend, whom I hardly knew, and her mother and father, whom I knew even less, already beside him. We all exchanged a chilly hello, but there was no movement to allow me to get next to my son.

They just told me his operation had been cancelled due to his high body temperature. They looked at me as if to say, "What do we do now?" At this point, I fled the ward. I was in a state of shock, frustration, helplessness, extreme anger, isolation, and I couldn't see where life was heading. I spent a lot of time walking around, not knowing where to go or what to do with my thoughts and feelings. My emotions, thoughts, and feelings were all screaming at me, tying themselves up like a headful of spaghetti I was struggling to organise.

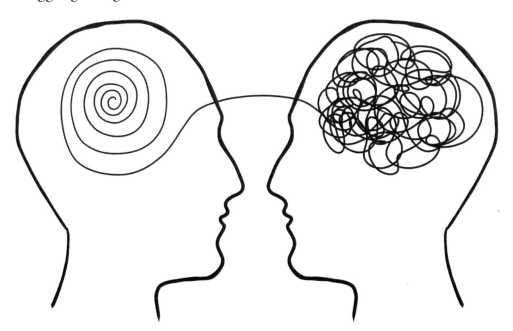

I couldn't get through to my husband on the phone who was at home trying to keep his business running. My daughter was nowhere to be seen. I had never experienced such emotional pain in my heart like this before. I truly felt there was no other way out of this pain but to release it through self-harm.

Thankfully, I found a bench in the sunshine. I shut my eyes, held my head up to the sun, and I breathed. I began to ask myself soul-searching questions to start understanding why I was thinking and feeling this way.

I almost chastised myself for asking such a stupid question.

It was obvious I was upset because my son's operation had been cancelled for the third time.

Is that all?

What else?

My husband isn't here with me sharing this burden. But I have my daughter, thank goodness.

Is this really all of it?

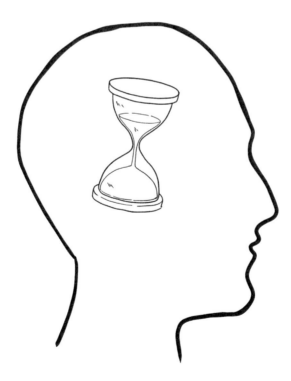

Okay! Okay! It's them! ("them" meaning my son's girlfriend, her mother, and her father) *They are here invading **my** space next to **my** son. They got here before me. They beat me to it. I hate them for it.*

OK, good. Why do you want to harm yourself?

Because I can't bear these feelings. I don't know what to do about them. It hurts so, so much. I'm frightened it will never get easier. I'm frightened about the future. Will my son be in ITU the rest of his life, waiting, seesawing between an improvement and then a downturn in his health? Will he live or will he die? Will he walk again, or won't he? Will he be back riding his bike again, whoop-whopping with exhilaration and excitement as he hurtles down the tracks in twelve months' time or will he still be lying here?

So, I then asked myself, what's the benefit of self-harming?

It will release the emotional pain. I will be able to breathe again. It will make me feel better.

How will it benefit your son, daughter, husband, and everyone else who loves you?

It won't, I admit to myself. *It will upset them. My husband isn't here with us. It will upset my daughter, and I can't upset her more than she already is over her brother. I can't look after them if I do this. My son and daughter need me here, right now. And anyway, I can't stand physical pain, so it will probably hurt more than the emotional pain I'm feeling.*

At this self-honesty, I saw the lighter side of the options available to me. I realized that self-harm wasn't going to make the situation any better for anybody, and it's only a very temporary release, not a long-term fix.

I breathed deeply, dried my eyes, and went off to find my daughter.

She was desperately worried because she couldn't find me. She expected me to be next to her brother. I had vanished, leaving her bewildered and upset, not knowing what was going on. I had left her to face her brother's girlfriend, mother, and father whom she didn't know.

This level of self-honesty made me face the music. It made me see clearly what the better option was for me and for my family, the people I hold closest to my heart. It made me see what I needed to do next.

Getting to this stage is a major breakthrough and means you're experiencing an upward turn in your bereavement cycle of change and loss and the five stages of grief.

Acceptance means you can now see glimmers of something better than what you had.

Step 3: Find a New Way Forward

Now that you have started to accept the difficult change you have been thrust into, you need to begin to find your new way forward.

Until you know this, you're not going to know what action to take, which will result in a lot of walking around in the dark, so to speak.

It's very common for people to know what they don't want – the situation as it stands.

Instead, you now need to discover what you *do* want.

Discovering this means getting in tune with all your senses, aligning them so you can get a 360-degree viewpoint.

It's possible you may need to step back and investigate all areas of your life and where you are today. Analyse the areas, look into your strengths and weaknesses, and rate them accordingly and honestly. What's working well compared to what's not working as well as you would like? And, of course, ask yourself a set of self-honesty-generating questions.

- What do you want to think and feel instead?
- How do you want life to be?
- Who do you want in your life?
- What do you want in your life?
- Why is this important to you?

This process may take a while, but once you have it in your mind, you will know what to do to start moving forward. Remember to write it all down, and be sure not to put any objections in the way. There will be plenty of time for objections later on.

When I finally realised I needed to change my thought processes over my dad's gender dysphoria, it became very easy to work out what my new way forward was going to sound and feel like. I finally had my objectives.

Objective 1: I wanted my relationship with Joan to feel easy.

Objective 2: I wanted to feel comfortable around Joan.

Objective 3: I wanted to be able to talk freely and be okay with using the different pronouns and her name.

This may sound weird to you, and that's okay. Many people tell me they struggle with this. At the very beginning, back in 1987, when my dad came out about his gender dysphoria, my Mum didn't want Joan to have the title of Mum. I can totally understand this, and I am sure I would be the same. It was her title and her's alone, so Joan became Auntie Joan. But for me, this didn't really fit the role she would be playing for the rest of her life, and I felt it demoted her in terms of her role within the family. I wanted to find the right title for Joan within my family. I eventually resolved to recognize her as my "other mum".

Objective 4: I wanted to lose that feeling of awkwardness, the uncertainty that was making me feel afraid of what other people might think and say.

Objective 5: I wanted to not give a fuck about what other people thought. It wasn't their life. This wasn't about them, but about Joan and me.

Objective 6: I wanted to stay feeling young and not go back to feeling twice my age like I had at the start of this process.

With all this in mind, I now had to start on my plan of action to get nearer to my objectives.

Stage 4: Time for Action

This stage of the process is exciting because you can be creative with your plan of action. You can think up the weirdest and most wonderful ways to start implementing your new ways forward.

Instead of making a list, try using spider grams to plot your ideas. You can get so much vital information down on paper and add to it very easily. This process is initially about plotting your ideas. Don't be tempted to restrict yourself with personal objections or things you have tried in the past that, perhaps, didn't work as well as you had hoped.

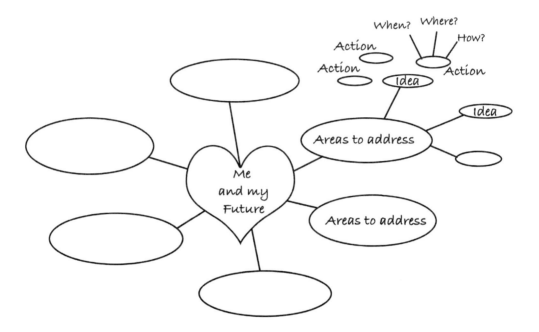

This process is very reliant on where you are in your difficult change.

For me, the difference between taking action to meet my objectives for my new way forward with Joan was very different from the complex set of emotions revolving around my son, his accident, and his girlfriend and her family. Coming to terms with my dad's decision was a long-term issue for me, but my son's accident was very new. As a family, we were at the start of this journey with no clear picture of where we were all heading.

This may be the same for you. Where you are in your journey is going to have a bearing on how much information you have, the range of new ways forward, and the extent of the action plan you can produce. Once this is defined, you can start picking which actions to implement.

To begin the 4-Step process, do the following:

1. Write out your objectives. What is it that you want to achieve?
2. Determine which objective you should address first.
3. Complete your spider gram.
4. Determine which action from your spider gram is going to give you the most benefit if implemented.
5. Decide how you are going to do this.
6. Determine how much time you'll estimate it will take.
7. Decide when you are going to start implementing this action.

Again, these are a lot of searching questions, but they are important to support yourself through this process.

When my son was initially in critical condition, the best support I could give was to be beside him as much as I could. Because of the work I did with my objectives and spider gram, I was able to realize that he was in the right place with the right people to care for him. I was there to support him when he opened his eyes to try to decipher what he needed between the strong medication and the ventilator. My immediate actions revolved around my mental health, pulling together as a family, communicating with his girlfriend, and sharing my time between being next to my son and still caring for my parents 288 miles away.

****

At this point, you have completed the 4 Steps to Emotional Freedom. However, it doesn't stop here. It's not a one-time process. This is just the first phase, and you will go through this many times.

You will start to implement your actions and use the self-honesty process to assess and analyse the results to work out what went well, what didn't go so well, what could be improved, and if you are still on the right track or need to make some changes.

Everything before this stage has been about being totally honest with yourself. Which, as I explained before, is hard. Scary.

Now you need to take the next scary step and start implementing the change you may have been resisting for a long, long time.

It is going to be okay. I am here to support you every step of the way. You may not feel it at this moment in time, but you are more resilient and stronger than you think. Let's face it, it would be so much easier to throw this book in the bin, say, "It's all a load of crap," and continue life as you always have. But even though you may be feeling challenged, you're still reading this, which shows you want to make a significant change to the way you are thinking and feeling.

I value and respect your decision, so continue reading and allow me to show you what these results look like in action.

"

As human beings, our greatness lies not so much in being able to remake the world...as in being able to remake ourselves.

— Mohandas Gandhi

"

Being In Action (Results Of 4 Steps To Emotional Freedom)

I have talked a lot about the steps you need to take to achieve emotional freedom. Along the journey of life, you will go through periods of time when you want to make changes, are forced into change, or want to resist the change and struggle with personal objections. Everyone is on a journey in their life, but it's how you adapt to wanting to make change and succeed – to come out the other side with a smile on your face, celebrating the successes in your life.

Does this sound good to you?

If so, that is fantastic to hear.

However, if you are struggling with personal objections, I understand that, and it's okay. You're not alone here. I have battled with my personal objections in the past and millions of others are doing so right now.

A 2023 survey taken by Champion Health states[4] "76% of professionals are experiencing moderate to high levels of stress" and "35% of employees report that the stress they experience at work is having a negative impact on them." What is even more interesting are the statistics for the causes of stress outside of the workplace:

---

4. Bliss, H. (2023, February 20). Employee wellbeing statistics: 2023 report. Champion Health. https://championhealth. co.uk/insights/employee-wellbeing-statistics/

Financial pressure 37%

Relationships 32%

Parenting 29%

Other 13%

Care responsibilities 12%

Ill health 10%

Bereavement 7%

Covid 19 5%

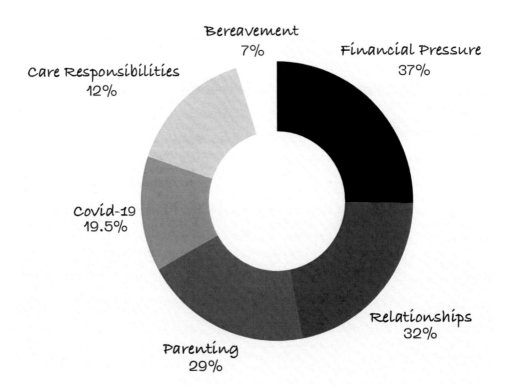

When you look at these statistics and compare them to the cause of stress that affected Vanessa, Georgia, Lizzy, and Emily, it was a combination that greatly impacted them.

During my working week, I speak to a lot of potential clients who begin the process of seeking the support they desire deep down. As we progress through our conversation, they share with me the pain they are experiencing. One thing I noticed was the more they spoke, the louder their personal objections became.

"I'm not emotionally ready to talk about this."

"My partner doesn't think the support I need is necessary."

"I can't afford to get support."

Then, there are others who state they will give it a go, but deep down they're not ready to fully commit to managing their change, even with the support right in front of them.

There are other times I speak to someone who knows their struggle. They verbalize they're not sure where working through their change will take them, but they are willing to trust their gut instinct, tell their partner their plans and why, and find the money to afford the support they need.

These statements mean they are ready to open their arms to support and work hard on making the changes they need to get to their emotional freedom so they can restore the happiness that has been missing from their life for months or even years.

This leads me nicely into reintroducing you to the four ladies who worked with me on the 4 Steps to Emotional Freedom.

Vanessa joined my program tentatively. She'd never had coaching and wasn't sure what to expect. She was a little nervous and found it difficult to put other things aside to work on herself. Vanessa explained she was still struggling with her mother's death and was now supporting her auntie through her end of life. On top of managing all her difficult thoughts and feelings, she hated her job. Thankfully, Vanessa was happy to talk about her negative thoughts and feelings but found it hard to reflect on and connect with what made her happy. She had lost touch with herself.

Many of my clients are in emotional pain. A numerical analysis of how strong this pain is doesn't really give me the information I need to learn about the depth of what they are feeling. Due to this, I have started using a colour analysis governed by my client's own imagination. I first ask them to describe in full detail the colour that represents when they have felt their happiest, then their worst time, and finally where they are now. The exciting thing here is every one of my clients described something different. There are times when the colours they chose had little relation to what we might automatically use to describe how we are feeling.

For Vanessa, this colour exercise helped her reconnect with wonderful past memories she had forgotten about. I was able to use her descriptions to support her through a breathing exercise which helped reassure her all these difficult thoughts and feelings are okay. This simple breathing exercise, using the descriptions she gave, made her feel great and restored her mindset to a more balanced equilibrium.

Vanessa now has two coping mechanisms she can use for the rest of her life: the use of colour and breathing to support her well-being when she needs it.

Georgia also had reservations about working with me but was willing to give it a go to see what came up. Even though she experienced high levels of anxiety and anger in the past around her family life, she clearly spent a lot of time working on these areas to make them manageable for herself. However, she was still struggling with feelings of wanting life to be different, being left behind, and managing her hyper-control mode.

As we worked together, Georgia reflected on how she put herself in this hyper-control mode because it was the only way she knew how to cope. She used it to manage the continual juggling act she was performing of looking after her own family as well as her parents-in-law and with a lack of support from other members of the family. This reflection was extremely beneficial in recognising what she had been missing. Georgia was now seeing her mother-in-law in a different, more positive, light.

Everyone views life coaching and other talking therapies differently. For Georgia, she was struggling with her feelings of betrayal. She explained she didn't like other people talking about her and, therefore, felt as if she was betraying her family with our discussions. Georgia also explained she was finding it difficult to manage the recovery process with her own mental health issues. It was creating too much pressure for her and the recovery time between the sessions was too difficult.

The clearer perspective she now had about her mother-in-law meant Georgia could go back to caring for her with added enthusiasm.

Vanessa and Georgia are still working through their first cycle of their 4 Steps to Emotional Freedom, but so far, they both clearly gained from the experience. Having time with someone to focus entirely on them, their position in life, and their difficult thoughts and feelings gave them the opportunity to start organising their train of thought and work out how to manage things more efficiently.

For Lizzy, a whole succession of serious family health issues quickly fell upon her, which didn't give her much breathing space in between. She controlled her feelings of anxiety and anger well with daily meditation and therapy work with others, but her feelings of being in hyper-control mode were extremely high. When you are faced with a father dying of cancer from asbestos poisoning due to his lifetime job and your son close to dying from a life-changing disease as a young teenager, you're emotional and mental well-being is bound to be stretched to its limits. Lizzy is a very peaceful person, but even her peace was stretched a few years later, after her father's death and her mother's serious illness.

Working through the 4 Steps to Emotional Freedom with Lizzy was an amazing experience. The colour analysis exercise gave her a very clear picture of her different emotions. On reflection, Lizzy found this exercise not only beneficial to our work together, but it has also supported her through her own work as a holistic therapist. She was able to refer to her colour analysis to support her well-being even after we weren't meeting anymore.

After one cycle of the 4 Steps to Emotional Freedom, Lizzy is still experiencing levels of hyper-control mode, but they have reduced greatly.

I want to remind you that our personalities are what make us unique to one another. After just this one step, her anger reduced to zero towards wanting things to be different, feelings of being left behind, and everyone being happier. This made me so happy to hear because the system I took her through was definitely working. As we reflected together, she also realized she recognised where the short bursts of anxiety are in her life and can now manage them confidently when they appear and let them go when it is over. Learning to let go and not hold on to unhelpful thoughts and feelings is a really important aspect of managing our well-being. Lizzy mastered this and has found emotional freedom from her past, her family, and her business.

Lizzy explained that even she was surprised by her level of anger at another driver in the hospital car park when taking her mother to an appointment. This was totally out of character for her. Life for her became easier when she realized she could be practical and give the support that came easily to her, getting on with what needed to be done. We also went on to discuss and work on her feelings for her son's decision to change gender. As a family, they all managed this change extremely well and were very accepting, understanding, and flexible. But, like most mothers, she found it hard because her son didn't talk to her about it and shut himself off from her.

The work we did together not only helped with her emotions around the bereavement of her father and mother but also the lingering, high emotions for her son's change of gender. This first cycle of 4 Steps to Emotional Freedom meant we could also talk about Lizzy's future – her family, her business, and her life with her husband. She admitted she still experienced short bursts of anxiety at very particular times during the week but could now manage them because she understood when they would occur and for how long. She now felt she was personally in a stronger place and in supporting others through her work.

Like all the people I worked with, Emily was another fascinating lady. At the beginning, Emily talked about her upbringing, and as one of the eldest of five children, she spent a lot of time caring for her family. With her father out of work and her mother in bed with a slipped disc, she soon took on the role of caregiver, taking over the helm. Her superhero mode was learnt at a young age and continued throughout her life. She became the go-to person for solid, supportive advice for family and friends, not only in crisis but also when a difficult decision needed to be made. This meant Emily's anxiety levels increased with less time for herself since family and friends were calling at all times of the day and night. She had always been someone who would drop everything for them, leaving herself behind whilst they progressed.

She talked about high levels of anxiety, being everyone's superhero, wanting things to be different, and feelings of missing out. Thankfully, she had been able to work on her levels of anger, which she had dispelled over the years. When talking about her anxiety levels, she explained in great detail how she would feel anxiety in her stomach. These intense feelings made her disinterested in food because her stomach felt like a washing machine, churning away. These digestive issues were a warning sign to me – there was a lot of deep-rooted unhappiness that needed to be uncovered. As the sessions progressed, a lot of uprooting happened. Thoughts and feelings Emily thought she had addressed, she was still clinging onto. We had a lot of fun unravelling these, and she worked really hard at addressing them and putting positive action into place to make life a lot better for her.

On reflection, Emily realised what she had been shoving into the back closet of her mind, and she understood the benefits of addressing them, not just for herself but for her whole family and friends.

Whilst working with Emily, all our sessions involved a lot of emotional untangling of those hidden, difficult thoughts and feelings that had been shoved into the back of her mind. Throughout the sessions, these would gradually come to the surface to be discussed, worked on, and resolved between sessions by her. By the time we came to the end of the first cycle of the 4 Steps to Emotional Freedom, Emily's levels had been reduced dramatically, but she still had to monitor her superhero mode, adding, "It doesn't feel as bad as it did." Meaning, Emily is in more control of her thoughts and feelings and how she manages her time for herself and to support others.

What I love about working with ladies like these is how our relationships develop and the sessions move forward. One issue for discussion becomes two, three, four, and so on.

I realise you are not Vanessa, Georgia, Lizzy, or Emily and have different issues with different levels of intensity towards your thoughts and feelings. Your life is real and so is what you're going through right now.

You may recognise some similarities in yourself regarding what you read about these four ladies.

Your experiences are yours alone.

Your thoughts and feelings are also yours alone.

Nobody is trying to take them away from you or make you feel as if you are unimportant. The 4 steps to Emotional Freedom worked for them and can also work for you. You can gain the benefits of this process just like Vanessa, Georgia, Lizzy, and Emily have done.

You can't go back and change the beginning, but you can start where you are and change the ending.

—CS Lewis

The New Normal (What Life Looks Like Now)

We all look at life differently. We all want different things, and no one way is the right way, but it's how we combine our lives with other people that gives it the meaning, the importance, and the value we're looking for.

Now that you have finished the first cycle of your 4 Steps to Emotional Freedom, it is important to process the information you've gathered from the experience. There's no wrong or right way, but you must reflect, analyse, and process so you can assess and compare where you are now to where you started, while still focusing on where you want to go. This is the only way to keep moving forward.

PREVIOUSLY-NOW-FUTURE

YOUR PAST

What does it look like?

What does it feel like?

What are you hearing?

What are you seeing?

What is troubling you?

What are you clinging onto?

YOUR PRESENT

What does it look like?

What does it feel like?

What are you hearing?

What are you seeing?

What is troubling you?

YOUR FUTURE

What do you want?

How do you want to feel?

What do you want to hear?

What do you want to be doing?

Who do you want to be with?

What are your dreams?

Before we move on, let's recap the 4 Steps to Emotional Freedom.

Step 1: Establish your self-honesty: Investigate your thoughts and feelings with total honesty so you can get a real understanding of what the situation is for you.

Step 2: Gaining Acceptance: Understanding your thoughts, feelings, and emotions will develop your acceptance and will help you see a clearer way forward to a better future.

Step 3: Discover New Way Forward: Explore what you want life to be like and understand the benefits it will give you and the important people around you.

Step 4: Take Action: Start to take action to make change happen for you. This is the time to plan and implement.

To stay in the driver's seat, I need you to consider a couple of points:

1. What has changed?
2. How are you currently feeling?

I would be very surprised if nothing has changed. Even if your personal objections got in the way of taking action, just investigating your self-honesty will have made a difference in the way you're thinking and feeling. However, this will also depend on how deeply you delved into your darkest thoughts and feelings and how accepting you are of what you have uncovered from your investigations.

Have you uncovered your pain points, and do you want to change them?

or

Did you uncover your pain points but you found them too painful to work with?

We all have different levels of personal drive for improvement at any time during the cycle of our 4 Steps to Emotional Freedom. This personal drive will either:

Get us on our starting blocks for change

or

Generate our personal objections

Where are you?

Sometimes we can be so fired up for change that we try and change too many things at once, become overwhelmed, and collapse under the pressure of it all.

Even though Emily and Lizzy found the 4 Steps to Emotional Freedom emotionally hard and painful at times, they still wanted to continue the process of making a significant change. They wanted a clear change in their thought processes and wanted to continue to work on other areas of their lives. Their personal desire for change enabled them to continue using the process to drive and strive to find the best way forward for themselves and their families.

Many people, myself included, can feel as if they are striving ahead, feeling a lot happier about where they're at. Unfortunately, the negative thoughts and feelings are a lot more in control than you think. This mindset can put you into a false sense of security, causing you to take your foot off the gas, saying to yourself, "Well, I'm feeling a lot better," but then continuing to convince yourself to prioritize all the other tasks you think you should be doing, putting yourself back at the bottom of the list of important people in your life.

On my journey to the emotional freedom of letting go of my victim mode revolving around my dad's gender change, I did exactly this.

To help me cope with anxiety and stress, I was offered six sessions of counselling from my doctor. In my first counselling session, I skirted around the subject of my life, flitting from one subject to the next.

During the second session, I finally said, "In the early 1990s, my dad transitioned to a woman."

As I looked at my counsellor's face, I saw the excitement in her eyes and interpreted it as, *My first client with transgender issues.*

My heart fell. She wasn't interested in my anxiety and stress issues anymore. Like so many people, she was only interested in the transgender issues and whether my parents were still sharing a bed – the private, intimate details of my parents' relationship. With this in mind and the dog dying the day of my third session, I cancelled. I began to have personal objections:

- My family needs me more than I need the counselling.
- Counselling isn't working for me.
- I already knew the real problem. I just hadn't admitted it.

But just like rehab, the first big step is admitting the problem, and that was a huge step forward for me even though I was only at the start of the process of my 4 Steps to Emotional Freedom. I had only touched the surface of self-honesty and already put up my defences toward how I was going to continue. I still had to address my personal objections.

Communicating with yourself is, first and foremost, the most important place for long-lasting change. When you can finally put your hand up and admit the problem like I did, you are at the start of and on your way to managing your 4 Steps to Emotional Freedom.

Once you have mastered the skill of practising self-honesty, the easier it will become to develop your communication skills with other people. But it takes time, patience, practice, and going outside of your comfort zone.

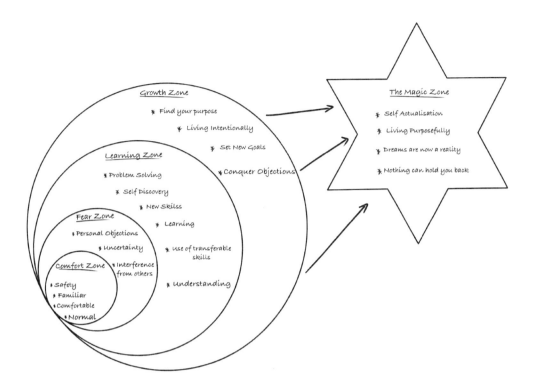

Going outside of your comfort zone, whether in your personal life, work life, or other goals you are striving for, can be very difficult and take a lot of guts to implement. But this is what stretches you and helps you grow to become a better individual in so many different ways. It will hurt emotionally and maybe physically. It will make you connect with your values. It will give you heartache, but it will also give you freedom – freedom to be who you really are, to be true to yourself, and live an authentic life.

For my dad to become Joan, he had to go through this process as well. He took the risk of losing his family, wife, career, and friends to finally be the person he knew he needed to be; otherwise, he may have "done something more serious to himself." Even though it was hard for all of us, I finally got out of my own head, connected with my own values, and let go of my ego. I am thankful my dad was true to himself and took the massive step to become Joan.

Before I could address the immediate issues when my son broke his neck, I had to first concentrate on my anger revolving around his girlfriend and her family. This anger was the most infectious of all my other emotions. I had to accept this young lady was going to be in our lives. On the day of his tragic accident, the first night in ITU, he proposed to her. She was not his girlfriend any longer. She was his fiancée, and I had to address this. At 19 years of age, she was young and very close to her parents, so they naturally wanted to be around to support their daughter. However, as much as I didn't agree or like the proposal of marriage, I had to accept it, just like I had to accept my dad's decision to change gender. This situation was right in front of me, and it was real, even if I wished it would go away.

As hard as it was, I started to look at the bigger picture – life is complex and needs to be investigated, addressed, and accepted.

I asked myself a few questions, just like I have been asking you.

How can I address my anger and frustration with my son's fiancée and family?

Who was the best person to go to for immediate and honest support?

How was I going to then implement it?

You see, my friends and family would listen and say all the things I wanted to hear.

"You're his mother. You're entitled to feel like this."

"Of course it's going to be difficult. You're in a very stressful situation."

This made me feel better for a while, but it wasn't addressing the situation, short or long-term. As much as I didn't want to hear the truth, I went to the nurse on duty who was looking after my son because she had been involved in heart-breaking situations like this before – families struggling with their thoughts and feelings and the complexities of all the other revolving influences.

When I explained my anger and frustration to this ITU nurse, what do you think she said?

She took me to one side and sat me down. She told me exactly what I already knew deep down inside of me.

"You know, you're in a really emotional position right now. I see this a lot. It's so easy to lose sight of the bigger picture at times like this."

As I sat and listened to her gentle, understanding voice, she continued, "The only way to resolve this conflict with her is to sit down and calmly talk to her. Explain your feelings and come to an understanding, a compromise."

She paused for a moment. "You need to find a way for both of you to have your time with him, a schedule that serves everyone."

What she told me hurt, made me feel guilty, made me feel ashamed, and made me feel selfish, but she was right about all of it. I had to step up. I had to put into practice everything I had learnt about myself when I was coming to terms with my dad's decision to change gender. I had to stop being the victim, be grown up, keep putting my hand on my heart and practise self-honesty and communicate. I had to communicate with my son's fiancée, however difficult it was going to be.

And so I did.

It wasn't easy for me or my potential daughter-in-law, but between us, we came up with a very simple visiting schedule. This gave us our own time with the person we both loved. It gave us a little bit of overlap time so we could get used to being together, and it also gave us the time that we all needed away from the bedside, which can be so exhausting.

It wasn't perfect, but it was a lot better.

We can't always make it perfect, but manageable is a great starting point.

And this is why the 4 Steps to Emotional Freedom is a continuous cycle.

The First Cycle:

As you work through this first cycle, you will investigate *what you are really thinking and feeling*. To the majority of people, this can be a tough question because they may have been spending years trying to put to one side what they are really thinking and feeling due to the pain. Nonetheless, it is a vital question to start asking, because until you know the answers, how are you going to move on to the second question?

What are the real issues? When we spend so much time trying to hide from the truth, we become experts in denying ourselves of it. By exploring what the real issues are, we are identifying what is urgent and important and what isn't. It is easy to put what's urgent and important at the bottom of our to-do list because it likely needs a lot of thought and perhaps comes with some hard decisions that may be emotionally painful to come to terms with.

However, when we have answered the first two questions, we get to a better place with, hopefully, easier questions. *What do you want to be thinking and feeling instead?* This will not only include things like your thoughts and feelings but also what mood you want to be in, the options available to you, reconnecting with your values, the people you want to be around, and what you want to be doing with and reconnecting to your skills and capabilities – all the good things you want in your life.

Once you have these in mind, how you start achieving them will flow naturally. You will see what needs to be done to have these things in your life and, of course, when you are going to start taking action.

The Second Cycle:

The start of the second and subsequent cycles begin in a very similar way to the first, by looking with self-honesty at where you are and looking into what you are thinking and feeling after the actions you have taken. You will ask the question, "Is this where I thought I would be?" You will examine what went well and what could have been done better.

When you're enthused with your new ways forward, it's very easy to put yourself in action. Often, we forget how much time everyday life takes up, and we don't get as much done as we hoped. This can cause us to feel we have fallen short of our expectations and then we disapprove of our performance and commitment. If this is the case, perhaps this is a place to be more realistic about your action- setting as an area of improvement. Whether or not you are happy with your progress at this stage, you must acknowledge and accept where you are so you can move on without affecting your future plans. Acknowledge and accept where you are right now and what you have or haven't achieved. Accept you are at the perfect place for you in this moment.

It is a good idea at this stage to refer back to overall goals and check if you are still heading in the right direction to set realistic goals to work through.

"How many cycles should the I expect to go through?"

The answer to this is vague, I am afraid. There is no "one way fits all." Various points will need to be considered. Some people only need support for a few cycles and can then continue to work on their 4 Steps to Emotional Freedom on their own. Others, with more complex issues or past experiences, will need more support. In other words, it all depends on the individual and how well they are managing their thoughts, feelings, and actions. Some need me to hold them accountable, and others have grown with the process to the extent that they have become motivated and can see their future clearly enough to hold themselves accountable.

So, what has changed for you now?

Whatever your answer is to this question, it is okay. You are in the place you are, and that can be changed.

However hard it is for you, it will get better. I promise that.

And I urge you to continue the 4 Steps to Emotional Freedom, otherwise, you will keep going round and round in a cycle of negative thoughts, feelings, guilt, regret, and victim mode rather than the positive one you truly want.

Growth is painful.
Change is painful. But
nothing is as painful as
staying stuck somewhere
you don't belong.

— N.R. Narayana Murthy.

What's Next

Having completed your first cycle of the 4 Steps to Emotional Freedom, you are now in a really great position to have a clearer view of how you want to develop with what you have already achieved. To keep making any great change, you need to keep moving forward so you can keep the momentum of your progression going.

The mistake so many people make is they get so far and start feeling a lot better, but find other things to distract them, putting all their good intentions to the back of their minds.

I don't want you to be one of those people.

I want you to keep the momentum going and keep in mind what you set out to do by keeping your vision for your future. By doing this, you will cement what you have already started instead of breaking the cycle and maybe even falling backward into where you have come from.

It is at this stage you may be thinking you are neither here nor there. You have started to move in a positive direction but still have a long way to go. The light at the end of the tunnel is getting brighter, but you still don't have a clear vision of exactly how life will be. In your vision, life can be different than reality. Following the 4 Steps to Emotional Freedom will help you to:

1. Assess where you are by practising self-honesty.
2. Acknowledge and accept where you are.
3. Plan your new ways forward to get you nearer to where you want to be.
4. Start taking action to achieve emotional freedom.

Assessing, acknowledging, and planning are just as important as taking action.

Why?

If you don't assess with total self-honesty, how do you know what you have done previously was right for you and your future, the best course of action, and if a slight alteration would get you to where you need to be far more easily?

It may be that on reflection, whilst practising self-honesty, you realise that, in actual fact, you have been looking at the problem, your future, or how life is for you now in a different way. You may have never realised this without going through the cycle. All of this is okay because when you work on your personal development this is exactly what it is all about – learning, understanding, being flexible, and finding the best solutions to the problems you are facing. You do it all day long but don't recognise it as a skill when managing the small stuff. This transferable skill can be sidelined because you go into a place of fear when something big is thrust upon you.

The learning process that you put yourself through during the 4 Steps to Emotional Freedom will not only benefit you for this problem but also for future problems. You will be able to look back with an open mind and notice how you used your strengths and how you adjusted your weaknesses to find a more resilient self. Each difficult change you go through will keep strengthening you. You will still feel stretched and out of your comfort zone. You will still have the influx of emotions and overflow of thoughts, but you will be better equipped to manage them all. You will know the questions you need to ask yourself to help you find your way out of the darkness, just like I had to do when I recognised I was at high risk of self-harm after my son's tragic mountain bike accident.

One thing is certain in life, it will always be changing. Some change will be fabulous, others will be good, and there will be some that will be horrific. All of the above is inevitable.

These dreadful times will make life feel worthless. The more times you go through the 4 Steps to Emotional Freedom and practice the described steps, the easier it will become, and you will find your normal.

Normal means usual for *you*. Everyone's normal is different. Life might feel worthless at this moment, but it's not, and in time, it will change; it will get better. Following what I have been sharing with you will help disperse these feelings, and you will begin to notice something better, more emotionally freeing.

What I do know is gradually, life will fall back into place. The change you experienced weeks, months, and even years previously will feel normal and not new anymore. It will stop feeling horrific, and you will be able to concentrate on daily life again without it feeling like a chore.

As family life progressed after my son's accident, our normal kept changing, and so we had to adapt. When he was in ITU for seven weeks, our normal was temporary because we knew it was going to change again. Travelling up to Edinburgh on a Thursday night and travelling home again on Sunday afternoon became normal. As we arrived onto the ward on a Friday morning, the ward staff would greet us with smiles on their faces, asking how our week had been. It felt good to be welcomed like this. This normal then changed when our son moved to Glasgow to the spinal unit. It was as if life had gone topsy-turvy again. A new establishment to get used to, new staff who didn't know us, a new routine.

But after a while, the normal began to set in again until another change had us back in Edinburgh whilst we organised our son's new home. Once in his new home, this is where we could really start to set the seeds for a long-term new normal – different, yes, but there was going to be no other way. We couldn't put life in reverse, so we all had to work on moving forward and looking at where we wanted to go.

Of course, we miss the pre-accident days. There are always going to be things you miss, but making sure you are in a place of no regret is one of the keys to maintaining your happiness.

The ability to adjust and adapt to change is so important in helping you keep in balance. My lack of ability and willingness to fully adapt and adjust to my dad's decision to become Joan left me with a mass of anxiety, stress, and huge imbalance in my life.

I want to be totally honest with you. As many times as you go through the 4 Steps to Emotional Freedom and reach your perfect life, you will still have down days – days that are tougher than the rest, but that's okay because the way we feel doesn't just have to do with our mindset but also our biological self, our hormone levels, and outside influences, such as the weather and other people's behaviours. What I can tell you is the more cycles of the 4 Steps to Emotional Freedom you go through, the stronger your skills will become and the more coping strategies you will have in your toolkit.

Tiwari and Deshpande state in their study on the effects of stressful life events on psychological distress levels[5], "The mental health of a person is influenced by both, biological and social factors. It is not a static condition, but subject to variations and fluctuations of quality and degree…"

If mental health isn't static, then neither is the balance of our well-being. It is the balancing act of our thoughts and feelings that are so important.

This is when we all need to have a toolkit of coping strategies we can use as and when we want to keep our happiness in balance. If you can feel yourself sliding down that spiral of change from happiness to something not-so-pleasant, you can look in your toolkit and find the coping strategy that is the most user-friendly to get you back up your spiral of change to your normal, your emotional balance.

---

5. Tiwari, SayaliC & Deshpande, SwatiR. (2020). A study to assess the effect of stressful life events on psychological distress levels of participants living in an urban area. Journal of Family Medicine and Primary Care. 9. 2730. 10.4103/jfmpc.jfmpc_96_20.

Spiral of Change

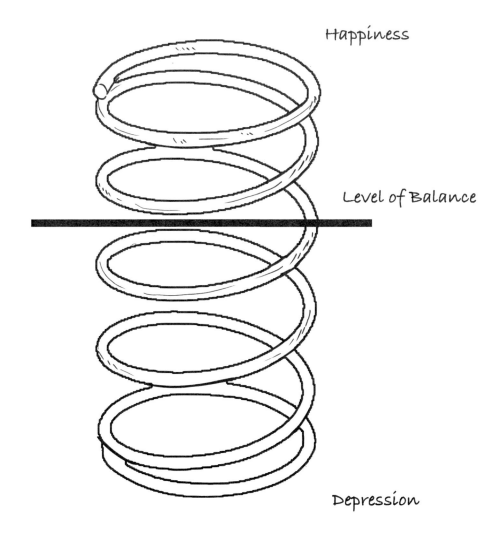

Happiness

Level of Balance

Depression

Your toolkit may look like this:

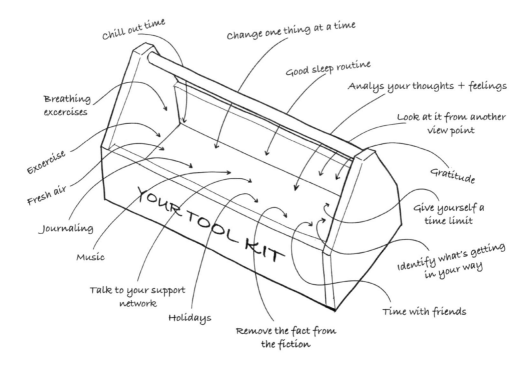

Some of these you will be doing continually and some you can pick up and put down as and when you need them.

If you are struggling or feel overwhelmed, that is okay. You are not alone. I still feel overwhelmed on occasion, but the key to long-term happiness is knowing what you need to do to get back in balance.

I know you can do this.

I know this because you are here with me now, having followed the knowledge and techniques I have been sharing with you.

I am here with you, listening to you, guiding you, supporting you, and helping you find the right answers *for you*.

Even though you would probably love to quit at times, keep going and never give up. I want you to consider this:

Is an easier life what you want or is it a better life?

A better life may not come easily, but don't you think it's well worth trying?

Whilst following the developments of Vanessa, Georgia, Lizzy, and Emily, you probably noticed how much they wanted to take control of the situation. This control is subconsciously put in place as a coping mechanism but can feel like you are hitting your head against a brick wall, trying to control something you have no power over. It's important to keep in mind we cannot control everything. Even though we may feel like it at times, the world doesn't revolve around us. Our lives are made of a huge array of small cogs. When life is running smoothly, our cogs are working in alignment with each other. They are in good condition, well-oiled, so to speak. However, one small change in life will disrupt one small cog, perhaps it will slip slightly or stick, making life a little off balance. A massive change in life will disrupt or even break many cogs, creating a mass of disruption in your emotions, feelings, and thoughts, which have an impact on your everyday life.

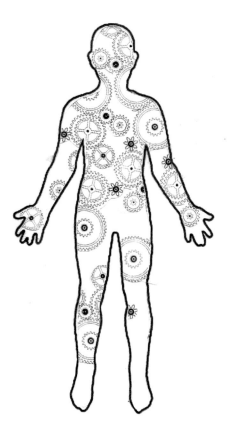

Following the 4 Steps to Emotional Freedom, one cycle at a time, will help repair these cogs. Each repaired cog will bring you more stability in life and the start of living your new normal.

In times of imbalance, like when our cogs start to break down, our concerns are at the forefront of our minds and can dominate every second of our day. It can feel as if the whole world is against us, leaving us with feelings that everything is out of our control. This is the exact time we need to step back and take a look at what we do have control over.

Levels of control can be broken down into three categories:

1. No control
2. Some influence over the situation
3. Total control

Perhaps a better way of looking at the sense of control is to separate the issues out:

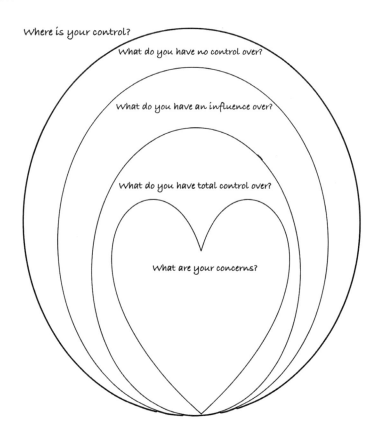

Where is your control?

What do you have no control over?

What do you have an influence over?

What do you have total control over?

What are your concerns?

First, note what your concerns are so you can see them clearly in front of you. They may feel obvious, but all these concerns will start to clog up your mindset. Start writing them down in no particular order.

Secondly, note what you have total control over. It may not feel like much at first, but thinking through your life, what you have, your transferable skills, and the support network you have will help you see you have more control than you originally thought.

Thirdly, note what you have an influence over. This may include other people, things, changes that can be made.

Finally, note what you have no control over.

What do you notice?

By doing this exercise, you will be able to see more clearly what is or is not achievable, and this will help take away some of the frustrations, anger, resentment, and anxiety around how you plan to manage difficult change in your life.

We all deserve to be happy. The problem is the thoughtless comments from those around us who are unaware of what we're going through that should have never been said in the first place. What is even worse, are the negative comments we tell ourselves we should have never actually entertained. They can give us a lifetime of heartache. I don't want you to entertain them any longer because entertaining them gives them more strength. Instead, I want you to use this book and make it work for you so you can live a happy, calm, peaceful, and brilliant life. You will become the person you know you should be by allowing the real you to come to the surface and flourish with emotional freedom, simplicity, and love.

"You must be willing to give up who you are to become what you want to be."

— Orrin Woodward

Conclusion

"The most beautiful and profound way to change yourself is to accept yourself completely, as imperfect as you are now." — *Maxime Lagacé (Canadian Hockey Player)*

There are those of us who think we are perfect and those who know there's a lot of room for improvement. There are those of us who can't be bothered to improve ourselves or don't know how, and there are those who do everything in their power to become the person they really want to be.

Who are you?

Whomever you are, it can be difficult to admit your failings, your flaws, and the mismanagement of difficult changes in your life. Maxime Lagacé's quote is the perfect place to start managing yourself. It can be a hard concept to admit, but once you put your hand on your heart and admit you're totally imperfect, you can start with a clean slate.

I was recently speaking at an event about the importance of self-honesty and was asked a very important question regarding what I am supporting you with right now.

"Cath, what was the difference between the time span of total acceptance with your dad's gender reassignment and your son's adjustment to living life as a quadriplegic?"

The answer was very easy.

To totally accept my dad's decision to become Joan, it took me approximately twenty-eight years of fumbling around with my negative thoughts and feelings.

The time it took for me to accept my son's life-changing injuries was five and a half years.

This massive difference, I could say, is due to the situations and my maturity. Even so, my developed levels of self-honesty made a massive impact on me. Just being able to listen to my true feelings, accept other people's honest opinions, and ask myself searching questions allowed me to stay connected with what I was really thinking and feeling. As a result, I was able to manage, and still manage, the many difficult situations I was faced with during my son's life-changing injury.

The power of self-honesty is immense.

I want you to be able to tap into the power of self-honesty so you can reduce the risk of more anxiety, stress, depression, and wasted years, unlike what I did.

I want you to be able to find your new normal so you can go about your daily life no longer feeling like it's a chore.

I want you to be able to end sadness, restore happiness, calm, and peacefulness after a difficult change in your life.

If this sounds like what you want to continue doing, then let me support you further to get to that place of happiness, calm, and peacefulness quickly. We will cement your new coping mechanisms in place and build that all-important tool kit. The tool kit is to be used as and when you need it so you are better equipped to manage the next change thrown into your life. There will be changes in your life, but knowing you have the coping mechanisms and tool kit will make you feel more in control and knowledgeable about your thoughts and feelings and what your body is trying to tell you.

If this sounds like something you need, scan the QR Code and connect with me.

Remember you are not alone.

"

When things change inside you, things change around you.

— Unknown

"